HEWLETT-WOODMERE PUBLIC LIBRARY
HEWLETT, NEW YORK

TERRORISM IN THE 21ST CENTURY: CAUSES AND EFFECTS™

Investigating the CRASH OF FLIGHT 93

LENA KOYA AND TONYA BUELL

Rosen YA™
New York

Published in 2018 by The Rosen Publishing Group, Inc.
29 East 21st Street, New York, NY 10010

Copyright © 2018 by The Rosen Publishing Group, Inc.

First Edition

All rights reserved. No part of this book may be reproduced in any form without permission in writing from the publisher, except by a reviewer.

Library of Congress Cataloging-in-Publication Data

Names: Koya, Lena, author. | Buell, Tonya, author.
Title: Investigating the crash of Flight 93 / Lena Koya and Tonya Buell.
Description: New York, NY : The Rosen Publishing Group, Inc., 2018. | Series: Terrorism in the 21st century: causes and effects | Includes bibliographical references and index.
Identifiers: LCCN 2017002346 | ISBN 9781508174592 (library-bound)
Subjects: LCSH: United Airlines Flight 93 Hijacking Incident, 2001—Juvenile literature. | September 11 Terrorist Attacks, 2001—Juvenile literature. | Terrorism—United States—Juvenile literature.
Classification: LCC HV6432.7 .K69 2018 | DDC 974.8/79044—dc23
LC record available at https://lccn.loc.gov/2017002346

Manufactured in China

On the cover: A memorial for victims of the crash of Flight 93 was erected soon after September 11, 2001.

3 1327 00657 6805

Contents

Introduction 4

CHAPTER ONE
Misinterpreting a Religion 7

CHAPTER TWO
United Airlines Flight 93 14

CHAPTER THREE
The Heroes of Flight 93 24

CHAPTER FOUR
The Passengers Revolt 34

CHAPTER FIVE
Responses and Aftermath 42

Timeline 52
Glossary 54
For More Information 56
For Further Reading 59
Bibliography 60
Index 62

Introduction

On the morning of Tuesday, September 11, 2001, a bright and cloudless day, the unthinkable occurred. Four planes were hijacked by terrorists and were flown into various targets, killing everyone aboard. American Airlines Flight 11 and United Airlines Flight 175 were crashed into the World Trade Center towers at 8:46 and 9:03 a.m., killing not only everyone aboard the flights but hundreds of people in the towers. Less than two hours later, both towers would collapse, causing a total of 2,753 deaths. The third plane, American Airlines Flight 77, was crashed into the Pentagon building in Washington, DC, at 9:37 a.m., killing 189.

But the fourth plane, United Airlines Flight 93, was different. Unlike the other hijacked flights, it did not crash into a well-known target. Rather, it crashed into a rural field in Pennsylvania at 10:03 a.m., killing all forty passengers and crew members aboard but no one on the ground. Soon after the attacks, investigators began looking into what happened on Flight 93 in particular. What happened on board that made it crash into a rural field instead of a target that could cause greater casualties? If the plane had been intended for a different target, what was it? And what had the passengers on board Flight 93 potentially done in order to change the hijackers' plans?

During the doomed flight, many passengers were able to call family members and other loved ones to tell them what was going on. Later, these calls, as well as interviews with those who spoke with Flight 93 passengers, would provide important evidence for what had occurred on the flight. Flight data and cockpit recorders found at the crash site provided additional information, including what was said in the cockpit minutes before Flight 93 crashed.

All of this evidence together painted a picture of extreme heroism on the part of the passengers and crew of United Airlines Flight 93. After

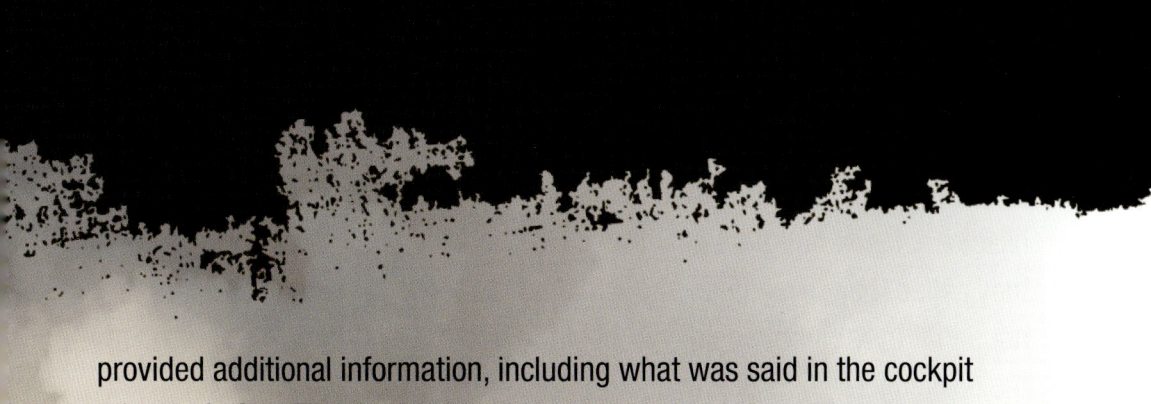

A couple looks out over American flag angels, representing each victim of the attack, in the rural field where Flight 93 crashed.

Investigating the CRASH OF FLIGHT 93

being hijacked and learning that other hijacked planes had been flown into the World Trade Center, passengers began to plan a revolt against their hijackers. Many of them knew that it was unlikely that they would survive; they called their loved ones and told them goodbye. But many also had hope that they could regain control of the airplane and fly it to safety. All of the passengers knew one thing: they would not allow the plane to be used in a terror attack that would cause mass casualties on the ground. Instead, they took action against their attackers.

One passenger, Todd Beamer, attempted to call his family from the flight and was instead connected with an operator. As he told her what was happening aboard the flight, he and his fellow passengers began to plan their attack against the hijackers. "Are you ready? Ok. Let's roll," were the final words he spoke during that phone call before the passengers initiated their plan. These words since became a symbol of the courage passengers and crew on United Airlines Flight 93 showed in a heroic attempt to save lives.

CHAPTER ONE

Misinterpreting a Religion

More than 1.7 billion people in the world follow Islam and call themselves Muslims. In fact, Islam is the second-largest religion in the world and the fastest-growing religion. Islam was founded in 610 CE by the prophet Mohammad in Mecca, in modern-day Saudi Arabia. He heard the word of God and had these revelations copied down exactly into a book called the Koran, which is the holy book of Islam.

Muslim pilgrims circumambulate the Kaaba in Mecca, Saudi Arabia, the holiest site in Islam.

A group of Pakistani men protest the killing of Osama bin Laden by American forces in 2011.

horrible destruction that was committed on September 11 by members of this group, the United States and many other nations have attempted to stop al-Qaeda from growing and committing any more acts of terror. However, that is not so easy since there are many members of this organization scattered around the globe.

Al-Qaeda had committed numerous other acts of terrorism before September 11, and the governments of the United States and other nations worked to stop their acts of terrorism long before then. After September 11, however, when the United States and other nations saw the high degree of destruction that could be committed by this and other terrorist groups, they worked much harder to stop al-Qaeda and to stamp out all terrorist organizations.

Preparations

The members of al-Qaeda prepared for the terrorist acts that they were to commit for several years before September 11, 2001. Prior to the retaliations from the United States and other nations after September 11, al-Qaeda had control of massive training camps in Afghanistan. There, al-Qaeda members learned how to act, how to go undetected, and how to fight when carrying out a terrorist mission.

Many of the terrorists who committed the hijackings on September 11 moved to America long before the event, living in hotels and rented apartments, trying to fit in while at the same time preparing for their terrorist missions. They were taught to fit in with Americans so that they would not look suspicious. They were often quiet and did not interact with their neighbors so that no one would know who they were. They shaved their beards, which are often worn by Islamic fanatics as well as many peaceful Muslims, and dressed in Western clothing. They were hiding in plain sight.

THE BEGINNING OF AL-QAEDA

The Saudi-born Osama bin Laden first began al-Qaeda, which means "the Base," in the late 1980s to fight Soviet forces in Afghanistan. This was part of the Soviet war in Afghanistan, during which Muslim Afghan warriors, called the mujahideen, fought against Soviet influence in their country. From this original goal, al-Qaeda was established to spread fundamentalist Islamic ideals across the world. It gradually evolved into an organization that aimed to wage war against Western secularism,

An Afghan mujahideen fighter carries a US-made missile during the Soviet war in Afghanistan in 1989.

or the belief that religion should not influence government, and particularly against the United States.

Some of the earliest attacks al-Qaeda committed were bombings detonated in Yemen against American soldiers in 1992, the bombing of the World Trade Center in 1993, the bombing of US embassies in East Africa in 1998, and the bombing of the American warship the USS *Cole* in 2000.

One of their main objectives before the hijackings was to learn how to fly commercial jet airplanes. Several of the terrorists enrolled in flight training schools, and some were seen by neighbors practicing flying commercial airplanes on computer flight simulators in their homes. Their neighbors stated that all they seemed to do all day long was practice on the flight simulators.

Finally, the terrorists determined that they were ready. The date was set, and their preparations were complete. We don't know how much each of the individual terrorists knew about what was to happen. They knew that they had been taught to fit in, that they had learned the skill of flying a commercial jet airplane, and that they each knew which city and airport to report to on the morning of September 11.

CHAPTER TWO

United Airlines Flight 93

While different terrorist groups have often used hijacking, or taking an airplane over by force, they normally did this to land the airplane at a different location. Then, hijackers would talk to governmental officials with a list of their demands that they wanted fulfilled before handing over the plane and its passengers.

On the morning of September 11, 2001, however, terrorists gave new meaning to the word hijacking. Instead of forcing the pilots of the airplanes to fly the planes to different destinations, the terrorists killed or injured the pilots and took over the controls of the airplanes themselves. The hijackers then crashed the planes into important and populated American buildings. Two of these planes, American Airlines Flight 11 and United Airlines Flight 175, slammed into the twin towers of New York City's World Trade Center. Another airplane, American Airlines Flight 77, crashed into the Pentagon building in Washington, DC. One can only assume that a similar fate was destined for United Airlines Flight 93.

The plans were all set in perfect order. The hijackers had been preparing for years for this moment. But United Airlines Flight 93 was the only plane in which the hijackers' plans were not carried out. What went wrong? What stopped the terrorists from carrying out their evil plan?

On September 11, 2001, hijackers flew American Airlines Flight 11 and United Airlines Flight 175 into the twin towers of New York City's World Trade Center.

A number of things stopped them. First, they seemed to be one short of the five hijackers that the other planes carried. In addition, their plane was delayed for over forty minutes, sitting on the runway of an overcrowded airport. Finally, the terrorists who hijacked United Airlines Flight 93 most certainly didn't expect the bravery of the passengers and crew on the airplane. From the very beginning, before the plane even left the ground, and before the fateful day even began, there was a series of mishaps.

The Missing Hijacker Theory

The three other airplanes that were hijacked that day each contained five hijackers. The terrorists are believed to have planned for each of the four planes to contain five hijackers, enough to kill or wound the pilots, take control of the airplanes, and guard the passengers so that they would be able to carry out their horrible tasks. However, United Airlines Flight 93 carried only four hijackers. What had happened to the fifth?

Some investigators believe that Zacarias Moussaoui was intended to be the fifth hijacker on United Airlines Flight 93, although this was later denied by Osama bin Laden. Unfortunately for the terrorists, Moussaoui wasn't around when the time came to hijack the airplanes. A few months earlier, at Pan Am Flying Academy in Eagen, Minnesota, Moussaoui asked to be trained to fly a commercial jet airplane. This was strange because he had very little flight training prior to that. In addition, he was only interested in learning how to fly the plane once it was in the air and not at all interested in learning how to take off or land. Moussaoui was intent on learning how to fly a commercial jet airplane once it was already in the air.

Instructors at the flight academy immediately became suspicious. Moussaoui's requests for flight training simply didn't make sense. Anyone who wants to become a professional airline pilot must know, first and foremost, how to take off and land the plane safely. These are the most difficult and important times when flying an airplane. After careful thought, the instructors at the flight academy decided to alert the FBI.

The FBI investigated Moussaoui. They asked his neighbors about him, performed a background check, and checked his immigration status. Although he was quiet and polite but not outgoing or friendly with the neighbors, the FBI was able to learn that he had recently purchased pilot

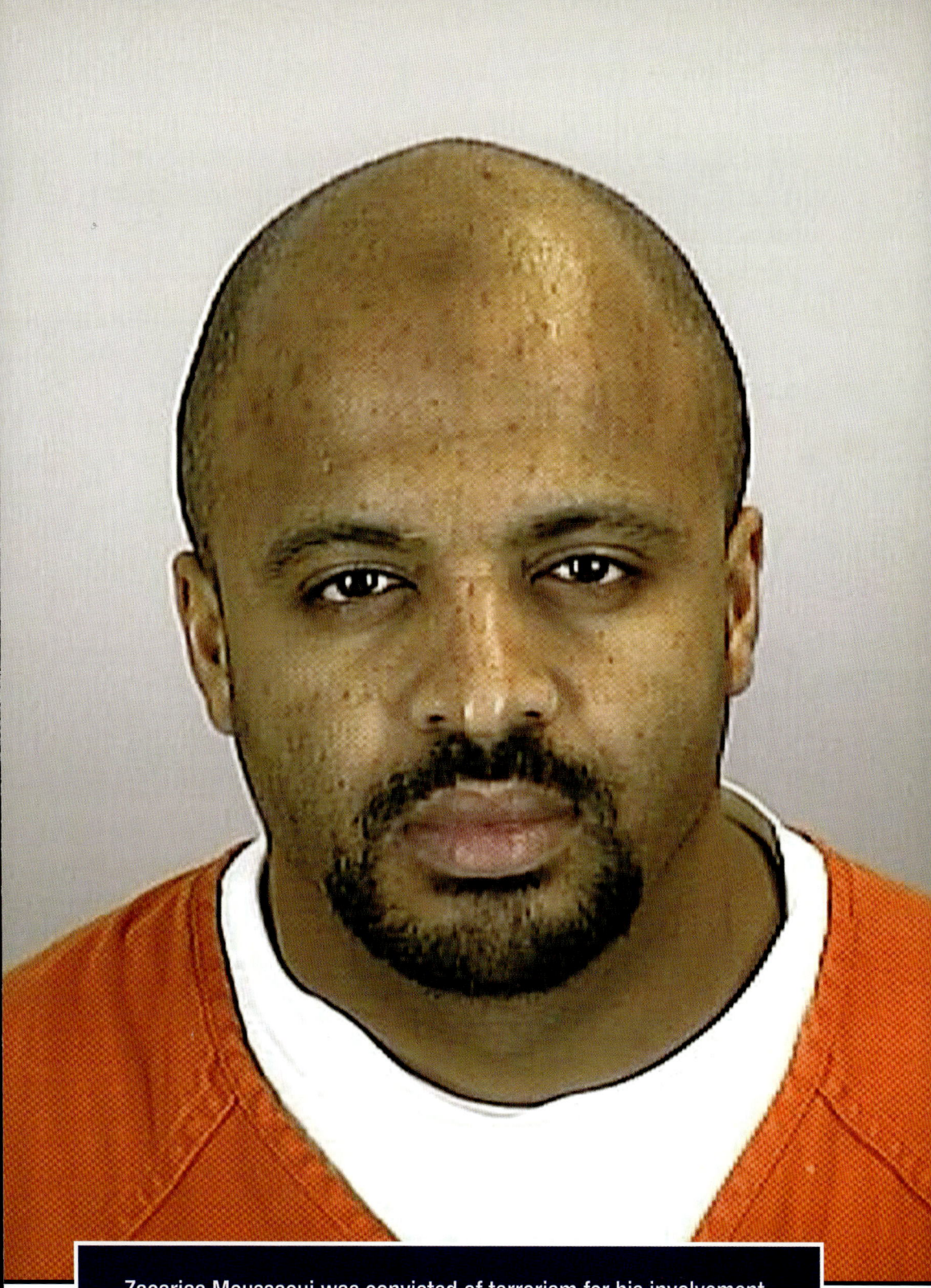

Zacarias Moussaoui was convicted of terrorism for his involvement in the September 11 attacks. He is believed to be the so-called "fifth hijacker" on Flight 93.

Investigating the CRASH OF FLIGHT 93

training videos. They also discovered that he was on a wanted terrorist list and that his United States visa had expired. The FBI immediately arrested Moussaoui and held him on immigration charges.

Another al-Qaeda member named Mohammed al-Qahtani was later suspected to have been the fifth intended hijacker on Flight 93. Al-Qahtani was refused entrance into the United States in August 2001 and was later captured by American forces in Afghanistan.

While we cannot know for sure whether or not Moussaoui or al-Qahtani was the intended fifth hijacker, many experts believe that someone was trained for the role and al-Qaeda could not find anyone else to replace him because he was detained or denied entry into the United States. Whatever the reason, United Airlines Flight 93 left the ground on the morning of September 11, 2001, with only four hijackers instead of the five present on the other hijacked flights.

Waiting on the Tarmac

United Airlines Flight 93 was scheduled to leave Newark, New Jersey, for San Francisco, California, at 8:01 a.m. on September 11. The terrorists had timed the four flights that they were planning to hijack so that all of the flights would take off at almost exactly the

United Airlines Flight 93

same time. This way, they would be able to carry out their evil plans before local or federal authorities could be alerted and before anyone could take measures to stop them. As soon as each plane was in the air, they planned to take over the airplane, turn it around, and crash it into one of several

Flight 93 left from Newark International Airport in New Jersey on the morning of September 11, 2001.

> *(continued from the previous page)*
>
> an additional screening check at Newark International Airport, but he was allowed to board after no explosives were found.
>
> Saeed al-Ghamdi was twenty-one years old and born in Saudi Arabia. He first attempted to enter the United States in November 2000, but his application was declined. Then, in June 2001, he successfully applied for a two-year visa. From the cockpit recorder recovered after the crash, we know that al-Ghamdi was at the controls of the airplane at some point before the final descent.

The Attack Begins

Finally, at about 9:25 a.m., fifteen minutes after both of the World Trade Center towers had been hit by two of the other hijacked airplanes, and about fifteen minutes before the Pentagon was to be hit by the third airplane, the terrorists on United Airlines Flight 93 decided to make their move. Passengers in first class watched curiously as those whom they assumed to be innocent passengers like themselves tied red bandannas around their heads. The men then stood up, rushed into the cockpit, and began struggling with the pilots. "Hey, get out of here!" one of the pilots shouted, a shout that was heard by the air traffic control center on the ground.

Captain Jason Dahl, the main pilot, had learned to fly before he could even drive. He and his copilot, LeRoy Homer, attempted to fight back, alerting air traffic controllers with the sounds of their shouting and the scuffle that occurred between the pilots and the terrorists. Unfortunately, they were not successful. Eventually, the pilots were overtaken and the terrorists took control of the airplane. They turned the airplane around toward a new destination: Washington, DC.

The terrorists rounded up the terrified passengers and flight attendants on the airplane and forced them to move to the back of the plane. They forced the passengers and flight attendants to sit in the last five rows of the airplane, rows thirty to thirty-four. The passengers and flight attendants were guarded by just one hijacker, a man in his early twenties who had a red box around his waist. He claimed it was a bomb.

Moving the passengers and flight attendants to the back of the airplane proved to be another crucial mistake. Formerly strangers, the passengers instantly bonded, talking with one another and discussing their current, terrifying situation. They talked about their families and discussed their various skills and options.

The terrorist who was supposed to be guarding the passengers apparently did not appear to be very threatening. He may have even left the passengers alone for some time. Whatever the case, the passengers felt free enough to talk among themselves, to discuss what was happening, and to make telephone calls from their cell phones as well as from Airfones, the telephones located on the back of the seats in each row of the airplane. They instantly began calling their loved ones to tell them what was happening, to find out what was going on throughout the rest of the United States, or simply to express their love.

CHAPTER THREE

The Heroes of Flight 93

It might seem like the passengers of this doomed flight were helpless in the face of al-Qaeda's evil pot. The unthinkable had happened: their seemingly normal flight had been hijacked by four terrorists who claimed they had a bomb aboard and had turned the plane around toward

Flowers and American flags sit in front of the Wall of Names at the Flight 93 Memorial in Shanksville, Pennsylvania.

The Heroes of Flight 93

an unknown destination. Even more worrisome was the news from the ground that two passenger planes had already flown into the World Trade Center. The passengers were stuck on an airplane flying 30,000 feet (9,144 meters) above the ground; they were trapped.

The passengers and remaining crew must have been terrified and in complete shock. What they had initially expected to be a routine flight across the country had turned into terror in the sky. Who could be expected to do more than tremble at the fate that they were about to face? What would you do, if you were faced with a similar situation?

Most people might shiver in fear or plead for their lives. In a situation such as this, many people would cry, pray, or do anything to alleviate their fear. However, as we take a closer look at the situation that occurred, and as we examine the passengers who were on board the plane that day, we can see that the passengers were actually heroes, not victims.

The Passengers

United Airlines Flight 93 was, by all accounts, the wrong plane to attack. In the terrorists' eyes, the passengers may have appeared to be a mix of women and the elderly, with a few men sprinkled in between. However, the passengers and crew of this plane were actually a fierce blend of activists, former law enforcement officers, martial arts experts, athletes, and airplane and flight experts.

One of the flight attendants had worked for United Airlines for thirty-seven years and was very familiar with the airline's and the government's flight emergency procedures. Another had been a flight attendant for more than twenty-five years and was also well versed in how to handle emergency situations. Yet another had once been a police detective and

A visitor looks at a display of the forty victims of Flight 93 at the Flight 93 National Memorial.

had trained and worked with the police force in Florida for years. She had only recently decided to change her career to live out her dream of becoming a flight attendant.

Among the passengers was a 6 foot 3 inch (1.9 m) rock climber who was formerly a prosecutor for Scotland Yard, England's police headquarters. In first class sat a 6 foot 4 inch (1.93 m) rugby player, who had once fought off an armed mugger carrying a gun. Across the

The Heroes of Flight 93

aisle from him sat a former college quarterback. One of the passengers was 6 feet 2 inches (1.88 m), weighed 220 pounds (100 kg), and was a recognized judo champion. One woman held a brown belt in karate.

One of the passengers was a weightlifter who sported a Superman tattoo on his forearm. Another was a law enforcement officer with the California Fish and Wildlife Department who had been trained in hand-to-hand combat. One passenger, a retired ironworker, had been in the military in his younger years and remained in very good shape.

One was a single engine aircraft pilot, who knew anything and everything about airplanes, according to his family. Another was a former air traffic controller with the Air National Guard.

There were a couple of missionaries, who would know how to produce calm in the most violent of situations. There was a tiny woman who walked with a cane and appeared meek at first glance but who was actually a powerful activist for the disabled. There was a football player, an avid baseball fan, and several business executives. The list goes on and on.

These were people who, on their own, would each be able to handle a crisis situation. Together, they formed a team that was almost invincible. This was not a group to contend with.

Investigating the CRASH OF FLIGHT 93

THE FIRST VOICES FROM THE PLANE

During the hijacking, twenty-six calls in total were made from the distraught passengers to friends, family, and emergency personnel. One of the passengers, Jeremy Glick, called his wife, Lyz, who was staying at home with their newborn daughter. He asked: "Lyz, I need to know something. One of the other passengers has talked to their spouse and he has said they were crashing planes into the World Trade Center. Is that true?" His wife told him that he "[needed] to be strong" but, yes, terrorists were flying commercial planes into the World Trade Center.

To commemorate the one-year anniversary of the September 11 attacks, the USS *Belleau Wood* displays Todd Beamer's famous quote.

The Heroes of Flight 93

Glick said that he knew that they were planning something, but if they were going to fly into buildings that would make all the difference. It was the first evidence that the passengers might be thinking of a revolt.

Another passenger, Tom Burnett, also called his wife to tell her that he loved her and let her in on their plan. He said: "Ok. There's a group of us and we're going to do something." His wife begged him to just sit down and not to draw any attention onto himself. He replied: "If they are going to drive this plane into the ground, we've got to do something."

Todd Beamer, who had been placed in contact with telephone operator Lisa Jefferson while attempting to call his wife, told her about his family, his sons, and the new baby they were expecting. He also told Jefferson that the passengers were planning to attack the hijackers. As Jefferson listened, Beamer spoke with other passengers about their plan. The last words she heard before he left the phone were, "Are you guys ready? OK. Let's roll!"

Final Phone Calls

As the hijackers scrambled to turn the plane around and head toward Washington, DC, the passengers and crew at the back of the plane used Airfones and cell phones to call their families and loved ones. Husbands called wives and wives called husbands, sending them final words of love and asking about the situation in other areas of the nation. Sons called mothers, sisters called sisters, and friends called friends.

Investigating the CRASH OF FLIGHT 93

Some of the passengers made more than one telephone call, and some remained on the phone for a very long time. Through these telephone calls, the passengers learned of the plane crashes into the two World Trade Center towers and into the Pentagon. They traded stories with one another, confirming accounts given to them by their loved ones. One man asked his wife to call the FBI, while another passenger dialed 911. A few of the passengers asked their loved ones if the stories that they had heard from their fellow passengers, about other planes crashing into the World Trade Center towers and the Pentagon, were in fact true. Some tried to tell their friends on the ground approximately where they were located so that law enforcement officials could be notified.

The passengers made a total of twenty-three phone calls from the Airfones on the plane, and many more were made from personal cell phones. A passenger would call his or her loved one, say a few words of

The Heroes of Flight 93

When passengers of Flight 93 heard about the attacks on the World Trade Center from their loved ones, they devised a plan.

CHAPTER FOUR

The Passengers Revolt

Once the passengers had voted, their path forward was clear. There were only thirty-seven passengers aboard and they had likely already discussed a variety of plans among themselves and with the flight attendants. They may or may not have assigned roles as to who would take what action in the hopes of gaining control of the airplane.

The passengers must have seen the flight attendants filling up coffeepots with boiling water, and the flight attendants must have heard those passengers trained in combat or martial arts discussing their skills. The business executives, or those familiar with organization skills, may have formulated a strategy and directed each person to his or her post or given each person a specific task. Because they were calm enough to discuss the situation and take a vote among themselves, they most likely would have been able to come up with a grand plan that all of them would follow.

"Let's roll!" is a common American slang phrase that can be regularly heard in action and adventure movies. These are the words of a military team ready to attack a target, or the exclamation expressed by a group of police officers preparing to capture a criminal. They were also the last words heard spoken to telephone operator Lisa Jefferson by passenger Todd Beamer. These were the only words required to get the passengers moving in their desperate attempt to overtake their captors.

This glass panel frames the view of the field where Flight 93 crashed in Shanksville, Pennsylvania.

Let's Roll!

One of the flight attendants had told her husband that she and others were filling coffeepots with boiling water to throw at the terrorists. The group of martial arts experts, athletes, and former law enforcement officers formed a team of makeshift commandos. They had spoken with their loved ones and had taken a vote. They were ready. At the sound of those famous last words, "Let's roll," the passengers began running over 100 feet (30 m) to the front of the airplane to break into the cockpit.

A few of the passengers were still on the telephone with their loved ones when the action began. "I need to go," said the disabled activist to her stepmother. "They're getting ready to break into the cockpit. I love you. Goodbye." The thirty-seven-year United Airlines veteran told her husband, "Everyone's running to first class. I've got to go. 'Bye." Another flight attendant simply screamed, "They're doing it! They're doing it! They're doing it!" And the judo champion told his family, in classic Arnold Schwarzenegger style, "I'll be back."

From the last words spoken to their families, it appears that all or most of the passengers and crew of the plane were involved in the fight with the terrorists. Final statements like "I've got to go" and "I'll be back" indicated that these passengers intended on helping in whatever way they could. Certainly, the passengers hoped to save their own lives as well as the lives of others on the ground. And, after hearing the last words that they spoke to their families, it appears that they truly believed that they had a chance of doing just that.

A Heroic Fight

No one knows, nor will we ever know, who did what or exactly what happened next. The judo expert may have used his expertise to take out one or more of the terrorists. The activist may have used her cane to trip or hit a hijacker. The flight attendants may have thrown boiling water on the terrorists, as planned. The large rugby player or the former football players may have struggled with the hijackers or pulled them from the cockpit of the airplane while the aircraft experts attempted to gain the airplane's controls. All we know for certain is that the passengers were in a fight for their lives.

THE FLIGHT 93 NATIONAL MEMORIAL

On September 15, 2015, the Flight 93 National Memorial opened to the public. It replaced a temporary memorial that had been opened immediately after the crash and was only accessible to the victims' family members. The new memorial includes the Memorial Plaza, which marks the edge of the crash site and includes the engraved names of all of the victims, as well as the Visitor Center, which includes an exhibit center, a learning center, and a walkway that follows Flight 93's path. In addition, forty Memorial Groves containing over 1,500 trees are each dedicated to a victim of Flight 93. The purpose of the Flight 93 National Memorial is to preserve memories of the victims and their heroic actions, as well as to protect the natural landscape and wildlife surrounding the crash site.

After running to the front of the airplane, the passengers broke into the cockpit and began to battle with the terrorists. A violent scuffle ensued, as the passengers tried to subdue the hijackers and regain control of the airplane. The airplane bobbed up and down, flying erratically as the passengers and terrorists each scrambled to gain control of the airplane. According to the cockpit recorder, "Give it to me!

Investigating the CRASH OF FLIGHT 93

Give it to me!" was shouted, apparently by someone attempting to grab the airplane's controls.

Local residents and air traffic controllers watched from the ground as this gigantic commercial jet airplane soared through the skies above them in a frighteningly unstable and volatile manner. That saw the plane bob up and down and from side to side as though it had completely lost control. They watched as the plane came closer and closer to the ground, and several local air traffic controllers evacuated their tower in fear that the plane would crash into it. They could have had no idea what was going on in that giant airplane in the sky above them.

The Crash

Suddenly, a loud crash was heard by residents of Shanksville, Pennsylvania, and all over the surrounding area. The crash was heard for miles. Residents in the area said that their houses shook, their windows rattled, and that it felt like a huge earthquake or tornado had hit their little town.

Tragically, the passengers and crew of United Airlines Flight 93 were unable to subdue the terrorists and regain

The Passengers Revolt

control of the airplane before it crashed into a wooded field in Somerset County, Pennsylvania, about 80 miles (130 km) southeast of Pittsburgh. All of the passengers and crew of that flight who had not already been killed by the terrorists, as well as the terrorists who had hijacked their

Investigators look through the crash site of Flight 93 on September 12, 2001.

A large-scale depiction of the interior of Flight 93 is on display at the Flight 93 National Memorial.

airplane, died in the crash. The heroes who fought to stop the terrorists from carrying out their evil plan gave their lives for many other innocent victims who may have died that day had the plane been flown into its

The Passengers Revolt

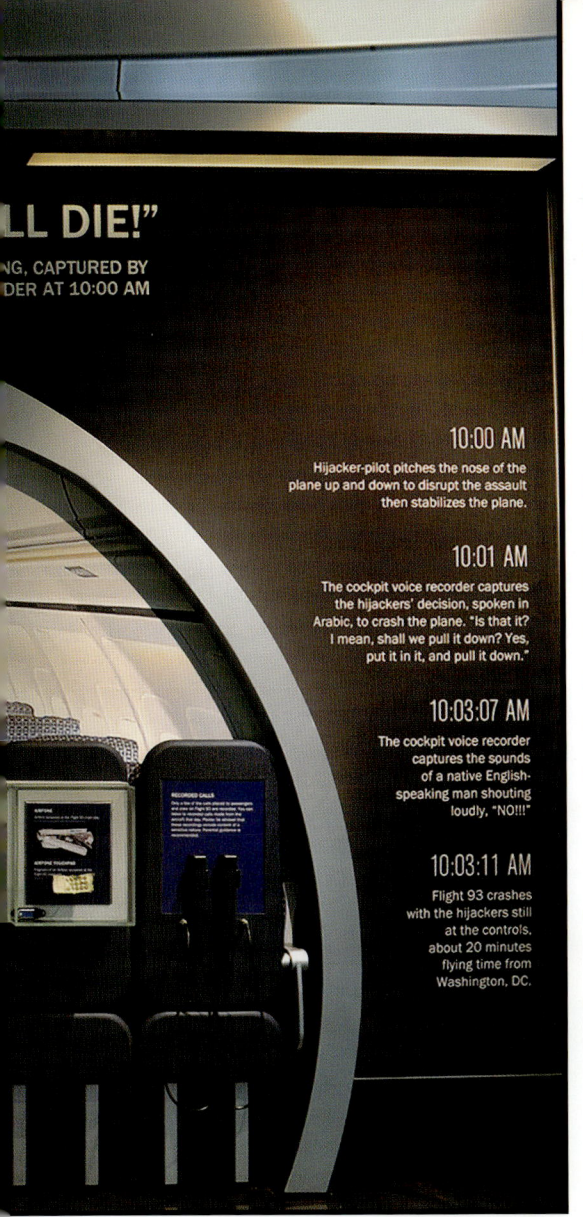

LL DIE!"
NG, CAPTURED BY
DER AT 10:00 AM

10:00 AM
Hijacker-pilot pitches the nose of the plane up and down to disrupt the assault then stabilizes the plane.

10:01 AM
The cockpit voice recorder captures the hijackers' decision, spoken in Arabic, to crash the plane. "Is that it? I mean, shall we pull it down? Yes, put it in it, and pull it down."

10:03:07 AM
The cockpit voice recorder captures the sounds of a native English-speaking man shouting loudly, "NO!!!"

10:03:11 AM
Flight 93 crashes with the hijackers still at the controls, about 20 minutes flying time from Washington, DC.

intended destination. They also saved one of America's precious landmarks and retained hope until the very end of saving their own lives as well. They were true heroes.

After the crash, the site was fenced off by the FBI so that the plane's flight data recorder, also known as the "black box," and its cockpit voice recorder could be recovered. The FBI also wanted to salvage as much as possible of the doomed plane, including the passengers' bodies and their belongings, and any other information that might assist them in their investigation. Within a few days, the plane's black box was found, and soon after the cockpit voice recorder was found as well. The analysis of these recorders, along with the analysis of the debris located at the crash site and interviews with the family members and friends of passengers who had had conversations with their loved ones, provided important evidence to the FBI in their investigation of this case. It also provided the victims' families with a more in-depth picture of what had occurred on Flight 93 during the final moments of their loved ones' lives.

CHAPTER FIVE

Responses and Aftermath

The loss of forty lives on board Flight 93 was indeed tragic. The passengers and crew were all special individuals; they had family and friends who loved them and whom they loved deeply. After their

A mother holds her son as they look at the Flight 93 Memorial one year after the September 11 attacks.

deaths, their loved ones mourned them and continue to grieve to this day. Despite their courageous attempt to save the doomed flight, they were unable to save their own lives.

However, due to the heroics of the passengers and crew on board the flight, a far more horrible disaster that may have occurred was prevented. Many, many more innocent people may have been killed had the passengers and crew of United Airlines Flight 93 not braved the horror that was before them. Had they voted to remain seated and be quiet, the plane may have crashed into one of the nation's major monuments and may very well have taken the lives of hundreds or even thousands of others. In this respect, because of the bravery of those on United Airlines Flight 93, a far more terrible disaster was averted.

Where Was Flight 93 Headed?

For many years, investigators were not sure where the terrorists who hijacked United Airlines Flight 93 intended to crash the airplane. In the years immediately following the attack, the FBI and other investigators concluded that there were three likely targets: Camp David, the presidential retreat; the White House; and the Capitol building in Washington, DC. However, Camp David is the least likely intended target because the plane was headed to Washington, DC, and not Maryland, where Camp David is located. Due to this evidence, and the fact that the president and other government officials were not often there, Camp David is no longer considered one of Flight 93's possible targets.

The White House, where the president of the United States, vice president, and his many invaluable cabinet members conduct most of their business, is a far more likely target. Either the president or the vice president, or both, would likely have been there on that fall morning, and there are numerous aides and cabinet members whom the president relies on for information and important advice who would certainly also have been there at the time. Also, since the White House is located in Washington, DC, where the terrorists had directed the flight, it makes sense that the terrorists may have intended to crash the plane into the White House.

The Capitol building, also located in Washington, DC, is another very likely target. The Capitol building, where our senators and representatives

> The United States Capitol building may have been the intended target of terrorists aboard Flight 93.

conduct their meetings and make laws, is a structure that reminds many Americans of the democratic principles of their nation. Many Americans regard the Capitol building as the place in Washington where our elected officials represent us. Had there been a meeting among the Senate or the House of Representatives, or both, that morning, many of our elected officials might have been killed, placing a deep wound in the heart of America.

Investigating the CRASH OF FLIGHT 93

UNITED FLIGHT 93

In 2006, the events that occurred on United Airlines Flight 93 were made into a movie, *United Flight 93*, directed by Paul Greengrass. The movie chronicles the final events that took place, including the passengers' revolt, in real time, using evidence provided by in-flight calls, interviews with family members, and black box recordings.
The film received accolades from critics and viewers alike, as well as support from many family members of the victims. In a review for the *Chicago Sun-Times*, film critic Roger Ebert wrote, "This is a masterful and heartbreaking film, and it does honor to the memory of the victims." It also received two Academy Award nominations for best director and best film editing.

According to the 9/11 Commission Report, published in 2004, bin Laden wanted to target the White House. However, Mohamed Atta thought it would be too difficult to do this and suggested that Capitol building might be an easier target. In the 2006 trial of Zacarias Moussaoui, more evidence was presented showing that the Capitol building was the intended target, including the fact that September was chosen for the attacks because Congress would be back in session after the summer recess. While the Capitol building seems like the most likely intended target, the White House cannot be ruled out because passengers calling from Flight 93 told their family members that they heard they were headed there.

An Unfounded Theory

Soon after September 11, several US and foreign news sources reported that a US military fighter jet had shot down United Airlines Flight 93 before it was able to reach its intended destination. If this were true, numerous questions would need to be addressed: Were the passengers of United Airlines Flight 93 actually the heroes described, or were they merely victims? Could the passengers actually have saved their own lives and landed the plane safely had the plane not been shot down? Should the US military shoot down hijacked airplanes?

Many people struggled with these questions as the news reports came out. There were reports by witnesses on the ground in Pennsylvania that a large bang was heard *before* the crash, and that a US fighter jet sped over the site just after the crash occurred. Other news reports suggested that a United Airlines fighter jet was on its way but didn't arrive in time to shoot down United Airlines Flight 93. Residents in the area also described burning wreckage falling from the sky, suggesting that the plane had exploded before hitting the ground.

However, almost immediately after these reports appeared in the press, Pentagon officials firmly denied that United Airlines Flight 93 was shot down by a military fighter jet. US Department of Defense secretary Donald Rumsfeld told Diane Sawyer in an ABC news interview, "The idea of the United States military going up and shooting down an American airline plane filled with American citizens is not something one contemplates." Several days later, the FBI, conducting its own investigation of the shoot-down theory, confirmed that there was no bomb residue or evidence of any explosive at the crash site. Furthermore, there were no reports of an explosion on the plane's cockpit voice recorder, which would certainly have occurred had the

A fighter jet flies just off the wing of Air Force One on the trip back to Washington, DC, on September 11, 2001.

plane been shot down. We can conclude, therefore, that the rumors that United Airlines Flight 93 had been shot down were just that: rumors and nothing else.

The War Against Terrorism

After the four planes were hijacked on September 11 and crashed by terrorists into various locations in the United States, President George W. Bush declared a "war on terrorism." The United States Defense Department geared up for an attempt to determine who was responsible for these horrible crimes and to eliminate their evil operations. Osama bin Laden was determined to be the mastermind behind the operation, and his network of terrorists, al-Qaeda, the ones who carried out these terrible deeds.

It was determined that Osama bin Laden and the headquarters of his terrorist network were located in Afghanistan, a country in the Middle East, south of Russia and west of China. The United States asked the acting government (though not the official government) of Afghanistan, the Taliban, to help them locate and punish this network of terror. But because the Taliban refused to help the United States, and instead were believed to be involved in assisting the terrorists to carry out their plans, the United States led an all-out war on the Taliban. The United States was helped by England, Canada, and several other democratic countries.

Eventually, the Taliban was destroyed and many members of al-Qaeda were captured. A new government was established in Afghanistan, a government that would not allow terrorist activities or organizations to operate in their land. The war in Afghanistan came to an end in 2014, although American forces continue to remain in the country in order to control ongoing terrorist threats. Unfortunately, in the years since

Investigating the CRASH OF FLIGHT 93

US army soldiers and Afghan National Army soldiers walk together in eastern Afghanistan in 2015.

50

Responses and Aftermath

September 11, the global war on terrorism has continued and even intensified. While many al-Qaeda members were captured, al-Qaeda still operates. Even more worrisome, a new terrorist group evolved from al-Qaeda called the Islamic State of Iraq and Syria (ISIS). American forces continue to battle ISIS globally, as ISIS has intensified al-Qaeda's strategy of attacking Western targets around the globe.

However, the first true soldiers in the war against terrorism were those passengers and crew on United Airlines Flight 93, who, going against rules that stated that passengers and crew should obey hijackers' demands, fought and won at least part of their battle. Although they were unable to save their own lives, they saved the lived of countless others on the ground who might otherwise have been killed on that fateful day. The passengers and crew of United Airlines Flight 93, who so courageously fought for their own lives and for the lives of others, should truly be regarded as the first soldiers in the war against terrorism.

Timeline

- **1989** Al-Qaeda is founded by Saudi Osama bin Laden to fight against the Soviets in Afghanistan.

- **1993** The World Trade Center is bombed on February 26 by al-Qaeda members; six people are killed and over 1,000 are injured.

- **1996** Osama bin Laden is expelled from Sudan and moves the al-Qaeda headquarters to Afghanistan. The Taliban gains power in Afghanistan.

- **1998** Bombs laid by al-Qaeda explode at US embassies in Kenya and Tanzania, killing 231 people.

- **2000** Two al-Qaeda suicide bombers attack the USS *Cole*, killing seventeen American sailors.

- **2001** Four planes are hijacked by al-Qaeda operatives and crashed into the World Trade Center, the Pentagon, and a field in Shanksville, Pennsylvania, killing nearly 3,000 people. In October, American forces invade Afghanistan.

- **2003** American forces invade Iraq.

- **2004** Bombs planted by al-Qaeda members on commuter trains in Madrid, Spain, kill 190 people; in a video, Osama bin Laden claims direct responsibility for the 2001 attacks.

- **2006** Zacarias Moussaoui is found guilty of terrorism charges in his role in the September 11 attacks and is sentenced to life in prison; al-Qaeda in Iraq is renamed the Islamic State in Iraq.

Timeline

- **2011** Osama bin Laden is killed during a US Special Forces raid on his compound in Abottabad, Pakistan.

- **2013** The Islamic State in Iraq renames itself the Islamic State in Iraq and Syria (ISIS) after joining fighting in Syria's civil war.

- **2014** ISIS gains territory in Iraq, and American forces begin airstrikes against it.

- **2015** The Flight 93 National Memorial in Shanksville, Pennsylvania, is opened to the public.

- **2016** Iraqi forces, with American aid, begin the offensive to remove ISIS from its last stronghold in the Iraqi city of Mosul.

Glossary

Airfone A telephone located on the back of seats that was used in most commercial jet airplanes until 2006.

black box An airplane's flight data recorder, which records details such as where the plane was located when it crashed, how fast the plane was flying, and other important data. It is made of material designed to withstand the most destructive crashes or fires.

Camp David The presidential retreat located an hour northwest of Washington, DC, near Thurmont, Maryland.

captors People who confine or jail others.

casualties People hurt or killed during war or military action.

cockpit The area in an airplane where a pilot and copilot fly the plane.

commanders Those who are in control of troops, particularly during a military operation.

courageous Brave.

erratically Not having any fixed course; following a random pattern.

heroic Having the characteristics of a hero or heroine; very brave.

hijacker Someone who takes over an airplane by force, usually with weapons or a bomb, and usually directs the plane to a location other than the one originally intended.

intended Planned.

Islam A religion that promotes peace, love, and kindness, and that is practiced by millions of people throughout the world.

Islamic State of Iraq and Syria (ISIS) The terrorist group that developed from al-Qaeda in Iraq following the American invasion of the country in 2003.

Glossary

mujahideen Guerilla fighters in Muslim countries; especially Afghanistan forces that fought against the Soviets during the Soviet war in Afghanistan.

Pentagon The building in Washington, DC, where America's defense and military actions are led. It is called the Pentagon because of its unique architecture, which consists of five sides, resembling the geometric shape of the same name.

rural In or relating to the countryside rather than the city.

secular Not having any religious basis or affiliation.

Taliban An Islamic fundamentalist group that controlled Afghanistan from 1996 to 2001.

terrorist An individual who attacks or harms innocent people, usually in the attempt to gain his or her political or religious goal.

For More Information

Federal Bureau of Investigation (FBI)
Department of Justice
935 Pennsylvania Avenue NW
Washington, DC 20535
(202) 324-3000
Website: http://www.fbi.gov
The FBI is tasked with both intelligence and law enforcement responsibilities and investigates national criminal activities, including terrorism, cyber crime, and civil rights violations.

Federal Emergency Management Agency (FEMA)
500 C Street SW
Washington, DC 20472
(202) 566-1600
Website: http://www.fema.gov
As part of the Department of Homeland Security, FEMA coordinates responses to all disasters in the United States that cannot be handled by local officials alone.

Flight 93 National Memorial
6424 Lincoln Highway
StonysTown, PA 15563
(814) 893-6322
Website: https://www.nps.gov/flni/index.htm
Managed by the US National Park Service, the Flight 93 National Memorial includes a Visitor's Center and a Memorial Plaza honoring victims,

For More Information

as well as memorial groves dedicated to the memory of each of the victims of Flight 93. The crash site is accessible only to the familes of Flight 93 passengers and crew members.

US Department of Defense (DOD)
1400 Defense Pentagon
Washington, DC 20301
(703) 571-3343
Website: http://www.defense.gov
The US Department of Defense oversees American national security and all military branches. It is the largest employer in the world and is housed in the Pentagon.

US Department of Homeland Security (DHS)
12th and C Street SW
Washington, DC 20024
(202) 282-8000
Website: https://www.dhs.gov
Created after the September 11 attacks, the DHS provides a coordinated response to potential threats against the United States and works in border and cyber security, as well as terrorism investigations.

US Department of Justice (DOJ)
950 Pennsylvania Avenue NW
Washington, DC 20530-0001
(202) 353-1555
Website: http://www.justice.gov
The US Department of Justice is tasked with enforcing laws and administering justice in the United States. It seeks fair trials and

punishments for those who are accused of federal crimes. The department is headed by the United States attorney general.

US Department of State (DOS)
2201 C Street NW
Washington, DC 20520
(202) 647-4000
Website: http://www.state.gov
The US Department of State oversees diplomatic ties with other countries and implements US foreign policy; it also advises the president on foreign policy issues. It is headed by the US secretary of state.

Websites

Because of the changing nature of internet links, Rosen Publishing has developed an online list of websites related to the subject of this book. This site is updated regularly. Please use this link to access the list:

http://www.rosenlinks.com/TER21/flight93

For Further Reading

Beamer, Lisa, and Ken Abraham. *Let's Roll!: Ordinary People, Extraordinary Courage*. Carol Stream, IL: Tyndale House Publishers, 2006.

Burnett, Deena, and Anthony Giombetti. *Fighting Back*. Altamonte Springs, FL: Advantage Books, 2013.

Friedman, Lauri S. *Terrorism* (Introducing Issues with Opposing Viewpoints). New York, NY: Greenhaven Press, 2010.

Glick, Lyz, and Dan Zegart. *Your Father's Voice: Letters for Emmy About Life with Jeremy—and Without Him After 9/11*. New York, NY: St. Martin's Press, 2013.

Greenwald, Alice M., and Clifford Chanin. *The Stories They Tell: Artifacts from the National September 11 Memorial Museum*. New York, NY: Skira Rizzoli, 2013.

Hillstrom, Kevin. *The September 11 Terrorist Attacks* (Defining Moments). Detroit, MI: Omnigraphics, Inc., 2012.

Homer, Melanie. *From Where I Stand: Flight 93 Pilot's Widow Sets the Record Straight*. Minneapolis, MN: Langdon Street Press, 2012.

Jefferson, Lisa, and Felicia Middlebrooks. *Called: Hello, My Name Is Mrs. Jefferson. I Understand Your Plane Is Being Hijacked. 9:45 Am, Flight 93, September 11, 2001*. Chicago, IL: Northfield Publishing, 2006.

McMillan, Tom, and Tom Ridget. *Flight 93: The Story, the Aftermath, and the Legacy of American Courage on 9/11*. Guilford, CT: Lyons Press, 2015.

Silverstein, Adam J. *Islamic History: A Very Short Introduction*. New York, NY: Oxford University Press, 2010.

Tarshis, Lauren. *I Survived the Attacks of September 11, 2001*. New York, NY: Scholastic Paperbacks, 2012.

Zullo, Allan. *10 True Tales: Heroes of 9/11*. New York, NY: Scholastic Nonfiction, 2015.

Bibliography

Barker, Kim, Louise Kiernan, and Steve Mills. "The Heroes of Flight 93: Interviews with Family and Friends Detail the Courage of Everyday People." *Chicago Tribune*, October 2, 2001. http://community.seattletimes.nwsource.com/archive/?date=20011002&slug=heroes02.

Breslau, Karen. "The Final Moments of United Flight 93." *Newsweek*, September 22, 2001. http://www.newsweek.com/final-moments-united-flight-93-151935.

Breslau, Karen. "Reporting on United Flight 93." *Newsweek*, November 26, 2001. http://www.newsweek.com/reporting-united-flight-93-149837.

Breslau, Karen, Eleanor Clift, and Evan Thomas. "The Real Story of Flight 93." *Newsweek*, December 3, 2001. http://www.prnewswire.com/news-releases/newsweek-exclusive-the-real-story-of-flight-93-74371102.html.

Dizikes, Peter. "The Mystery of Flight 93." ABC News, September 13, 2001. http://s3.amazonaws.com/911timeline/2001/abcnews091301.html.

Dizikes, Peter. "The Pennsylvania Crash: What Happened?" ABC News, September 12, 2001. http://abcnews.go.com/US/story?id=92517&page=1.

Internet Movie Database. "Flight 93 (2006)." Retrieved December 15, 2016. http://www.imdb.com/title/tt0481522.

Isikoff, Michael, and Daniel Klaidman. "A Matter of Missed Signals." *Newsweek*, December 24, 2001. http://www.newsweek.com/matter-missed-signals-148445.

Johnson, Kevin, and Alan Levin. "Recorder Catchers Passengers' Fight with Hijackers." *USA Today*, October 3, 2001. http://usatoday30.usatoday.com/news/sept11/2001/10/04/cockpit.htm.

Bibliography

Morgan, David. "Flight Data Recorder Found at Pennsylvania Crash Site." Reuters News Service, September 13, 2001. http://www.reuters.com.

The National Commission on Terrorist Attacks Upon the United States. "The 9/11 Commission Report." July 22, 2004. https://9-11commission.gov/report/911Report.pdf.

National Park Service, US Department of the Interior. "Flight 93: National Memorial Pennsylvania." https://www.nps.gov/flni/index.htm.

Newsweek. "Living Through 9/11: Phoning Home from Flight 93." September 11, 2016. http://www.newsweek.com/living-through-911-496932.

Vulliamy, Ed. "Let's Roll ... ." *Observer*, December 2, 2001. https://www.theguardian.com/world/2001/dec/02/september11.terrorism1.

Index

A
American Airlines Flight 11, 4, 14, 20
American Airlines Flight 77, 4, 14
Atta, Mohamed, 21, 46

B
Beamer, Todd, 6, 29, 34
bin Laden, Osama, 9, 12, 16, 46, 49
Burnett, Tom, 29
Bush, George W., 49

C
Camp David, as possible original target, 43
Capitol building, as possible original target, 43, 44–45, 46

D
Dahl, Jason, 22–23

F
FBI, 16–18, 30, 41, 43
Flight 93 National Memorial, 37

G
Ghamdi, Saeed al-, 22
Glick, Jeremy, 28–29

H
Haznawi, Ahmed al-, 21–22
Homer, LeRoy, 22–23

I
Islam, overview of, 7–8

J
Jarrah, Ziad, 21
Jefferson, Lisa, 29, 34

M
missing hijacker theory, 16–18
Moussaoui, Zacarias, 16–18, 46

N
Nami, Ahmed al-, 21
9/11 Commission Report, 46

P
Pentagon, 4, 14, 22, 30

Q
Qaeda, al-, 9–13, 18, 21, 24, 49, 51
Qahtani, Mohammed al-, 18

R
religious extremists, explanation of, 8–9

Index

T
Taliban, 49
terrorism
  explanation of, 9
  war on, 49–51

U
United Airlines Flight 93
  crash of, 38–41
  four hijackers of, 21–22
  original target, 43–46
  passengers revolt, 34–38
  phone calls made from, 4, 23, 28–32
United Airlines Flight 175, 4, 14, 20
United Flight 93, 46
US embassies, bombing of, 13
USS Cole, 13

W
White House, as possible original target, 43–44, 46
World Trade Center, 4, 6, 13, 14, 20, 22, 25, 28, 30

AUG 2 2 2018

HEWLETT-WOODMERE PUBLIC LIBRARY

3 1327 00657 6805

28 DAY BOOK

Hewlett-Woodmere Public Library
Hewlett, New York 11557

Business Phone 516-374-1967
Recorded Announcements 516-374-1667
Website www.hwpl.org